ISBN: 9781729115022

Whisky Logbook
Probably the best grown up drink in the world

A logbook of 100 Pages 8.5" x 11"

Whisky Index

1	2	3	4
5	6	7	8
9	10	11	12
13	14	15	16
17	18	19	20
21	22	23	24
25	26	27	28
29	30	31	32
33	34	35	36
37	38	39	40
41	42	43	44
45	46	47	48
49	50	51	52
53	54	55	56
57	58	59	60
61	62	63	64
65	66	67	68
69	70	71	72
73	74	75	76
77	78	79	80
81	82	83	84
85	86	87	88
89	90	91	92
93	94	95	96
97	98	99	100

Whisky Name:					
Type [x]:	Scotch [ ]	Irish [ ]	Other [ ]	Single Malt [ ]	Blend [ ]
	Bourbon [ ]	Rye [ ]	Single Pot [ ]	Corn [ ]	Barley [ ]
Region / Country:					
Distillery:					
Age:					
Strength %:					
Testing Date:					
Details:					

Whisky Name:					
Type [x]:	Scotch [ ]	Irish [ ]	Other [ ]	Single Malt [ ]	Blend [ ]
	Bourbon [ ]	Rye [ ]	Single Pot [ ]	Corn [ ]	Barley [ ]
Region / Country:					
Distillery:					
Age:					
Strength %:					
Testing Date:					
Details:					

Whisky Name:						
Type [x]:	Scotch [ ]	Irish [ ]	Other [ ]	Single Malt [ ]	Blend [ ]	
	Bourbon [ ]	Rye [ ]	Single Pot [ ]	Corn [ ]	Barley [ ]	
Region / Country:						
Distillery:						
Age:						
Strength %:						
Testing Date:						
Details:						

Whisky Name:					
Type [x]:	Scotch [ ]	Irish [ ]	Other [ ]	Single Malt [ ]	Blend [ ]
	Bourbon [ ]	Rye [ ]	Single Pot [ ]	Corn [ ]	Barley [ ]
Region / Country:					
Distillery:					
Age:					
Strength %:					
Testing Date:					
Details:					

Whisky Name:						
Type [x]:	Scotch [ ]	Irish [ ]	Other [ ]	Single Malt [ ]		Blend [ ]
	Bourbon [ ]	Rye [ ]	Single Pot [ ]	Corn [ ]		Barley [ ]
Region / Country:						
Distillery:						
Age:						
Strength %:						
Testing Date:						
Details:						

Whisky Name:					
Type [x]:	Scotch [ ]	Irish [ ]	Other [ ]	Single Malt [ ]	Blend [ ]
	Bourbon [ ]	Rye [ ]	Single Pot [ ]	Corn [ ]	Barley [ ]
Region / Country:					
Distillery:					
Age:					
Strength %:					
Testing Date:					
Details:					

Whisky Name:					
Type [x]:	Scotch [ ]	Irish [ ]	Other [ ]	Single Malt [ ]	Blend [ ]
	Bourbon [ ]	Rye [ ]	Single Pot [ ]	Corn [ ]	Barley [ ]
Region / Country:					
Distillery:					
Age:					
Strength %:					
Testing Date:					
Details:					

Whisky Name:					
Type [x]:	Scotch [ ]	Irish [ ]	Other [ ]	Single Malt [ ]	Blend [ ]
	Bourbon [ ]	Rye [ ]	Single Pot [ ]	Corn [ ]	Barley [ ]
Region / Country:					
Distillery:					
Age:					
Strength %:					
Testing Date:					
Details:					

Whisky Name:						
Type [x]:	Scotch [ ]	Irish [ ]	Other [ ]	Single Malt [ ]	Blend [ ]	
	Bourbon [ ]	Rye [ ]	Single Pot [ ]	Corn [ ]	Barley [ ]	
Region / Country:						
Distillery:						
Age:						
Strength %:						
Testing Date:						
Details:						

Whisky Name:					
Type [x]:	Scotch [ ]	Irish [ ]	Other [ ]	Single Malt [ ]	Blend [ ]
	Bourbon [ ]	Rye [ ]	Single Pot [ ]	Corn [ ]	Barley [ ]
Region / Country:					
Distillery:					
Age:					
Strength %:					
Testing Date:					
Details:					

Whisky Name:					
Type [x]:	Scotch [ ]	Irish [ ]	Other [ ]	Single Malt [ ]	Blend [ ]
	Bourbon [ ]	Rye [ ]	Single Pot [ ]	Corn [ ]	Barley [ ]
Region / Country:					
Distillery:					
Age:					
Strength %:					
Testing Date:					
Details:					

Whisky Name:						
Type [x]:	Scotch [ ]	Irish [ ]	Other [ ]	Single Malt [ ]		Blend [ ]
	Bourbon [ ]	Rye [ ]	Single Pot [ ]	Corn [ ]		Barley [ ]
Region / Country:						
Distillery:						
Age:						
Strength %:						
Testing Date:						
Details:						

Whisky Name:					
Type [x]:	Scotch [ ]	Irish [ ]	Other [ ]	Single Malt [ ]	Blend [ ]
	Bourbon [ ]	Rye [ ]	Single Pot [ ]	Corn [ ]	Barley [ ]
Region / Country:					
Distillery:					
Age:					
Strength %:					
Testing Date:					
Details:					

16

Whisky Name:					
Type [x]:	Scotch [ ]	Irish [ ]	Other [ ]	Single Malt [ ]	Blend [ ]
	Bourbon [ ]	Rye [ ]	Single Pot [ ]	Corn [ ]	Barley [ ]
Region / Country:					
Distillery:					
Age:					
Strength %:					
Testing Date:					
Details:					

Whisky Name:					
Type [x]:	Scotch [ ]	Irish [ ]	Other [ ]	Single Malt [ ]	Blend [ ]
	Bourbon [ ]	Rye [ ]	Single Pot [ ]	Corn [ ]	Barley [ ]
Region / Country:					
Distillery:					
Age:					
Strength %:					
Testing Date:					
Details:					

Whisky Name:						
Type [x]:	Scotch [ ]	Irish [ ]	Other [ ]	Single Malt [ ]		Blend [ ]
	Bourbon [ ]	Rye [ ]	Single Pot [ ]	Corn [ ]		Barley [ ]
Region / Country:						
Distillery:						
Age:						
Strength %:						
Testing Date:						
Details:						

Whisky Name:					
Type [x]:	Scotch [ ]	Irish [ ]	Other [ ]	Single Malt [ ]	Blend [ ]
	Bourbon [ ]	Rye [ ]	Single Pot [ ]	Corn [ ]	Barley [ ]
Region / Country:					
Distillery:					
Age:					
Strength %:					
Testing Date:					
Details:					

Whisky Name:					
Type [x]:	Scotch [ ]	Irish [ ]	Other [ ]	Single Malt [ ]	Blend [ ]
	Bourbon [ ]	Rye [ ]	Single Pot [ ]	Corn [ ]	Barley [ ]
Region / Country:					
Distillery:					
Age:					
Strength %:					
Testing Date:					
Details:					

Whisky Name:					
Type [x]:	Scotch [ ]	Irish [ ]	Other [ ]	Single Malt [ ]	Blend [ ]
	Bourbon [ ]	Rye [ ]	Single Pot [ ]	Corn [ ]	Barley [ ]
Region / Country:					
Distillery:					
Age:					
Strength %:					
Testing Date:					
Details:					

Whisky Name:					
Type [x]:	Scotch [ ]	Irish [ ]	Other [ ]	Single Malt [ ]	Blend [ ]
	Bourbon [ ]	Rye [ ]	Single Pot [ ]	Corn [ ]	Barley [ ]
Region / Country:					
Distillery:					
Age:					
Strength %:					
Testing Date:					
Details:					

Whisky Name:						
Type [x]:	Scotch [ ]	Irish [ ]	Other [ ]	Single Malt [ ]		Blend [ ]
	Bourbon [ ]	Rye [ ]	Single Pot [ ]	Corn [ ]		Barley [ ]
Region / Country:						
Distillery:						
Age:						
Strength %:						
Testing Date:						
Details:						

Whisky Name:					
Type [x]:	Scotch [ ]	Irish [ ]	Other [ ]	Single Malt [ ]	Blend [ ]
	Bourbon [ ]	Rye [ ]	Single Pot [ ]	Corn [ ]	Barley [ ]
Region / Country:					
Distillery:					
Age:					
Strength %:					
Testing Date:					
Details:					

Whisky Name:					
Type [x]:	Scotch [ ]	Irish [ ]	Other [ ]	Single Malt [ ]	Blend [ ]
	Bourbon [ ]	Rye [ ]	Single Pot [ ]	Corn [ ]	Barley [ ]
Region / Country:					
Distillery:					
Age:					
Strength %:					
Testing Date:					
Details:					

Whisky Name:					
Type [x]:	Scotch [ ]	Irish [ ]	Other [ ]	Single Malt [ ]	Blend [ ]
	Bourbon [ ]	Rye [ ]	Single Pot [ ]	Corn [ ]	Barley [ ]
Region / Country:					
Distillery:					
Age:					
Strength %:					
Testing Date:					
Details:					

Whisky Name:					
Type [x]:	Scotch [ ]	Irish [ ]	Other [ ]	Single Malt [ ]	Blend [ ]
	Bourbon [ ]	Rye [ ]	Single Pot [ ]	Corn [ ]	Barley [ ]
Region / Country:					
Distillery:					
Age:					
Strength %:					
Testing Date:					
Details:					

Whisky Name:					
Type [x]:	Scotch [ ]	Irish [ ]	Other [ ]	Single Malt [ ]	Blend [ ]
	Bourbon [ ]	Rye [ ]	Single Pot [ ]	Corn [ ]	Barley [ ]
Region / Country:					
Distillery:					
Age:					
Strength %:					
Testing Date:					
Details:					

Whisky Name:					
Type [x]:	Scotch [ ]	Irish [ ]	Other [ ]	Single Malt [ ]	Blend [ ]
	Bourbon [ ]	Rye [ ]	Single Pot [ ]	Corn [ ]	Barley [ ]
Region / Country:					
Distillery:					
Age:					
Strength %:					
Testing Date:					
Details:					

Whisky Name:					
Type [x]:	Scotch [ ]	Irish [ ]	Other [ ]	Single Malt [ ]	Blend [ ]
	Bourbon [ ]	Rye [ ]	Single Pot [ ]	Corn [ ]	Barley [ ]
Region / Country:					
Distillery:					
Age:					
Strength %:					
Testing Date:					
Details:					

Whisky Name:					
Type [x]:	Scotch [ ]	Irish [ ]	Other [ ]	Single Malt [ ]	Blend [ ]
	Bourbon [ ]	Rye [ ]	Single Pot [ ]	Corn [ ]	Barley [ ]
Region / Country:					
Distillery:					
Age:					
Strength %:					
Testing Date:					
Details:					

Whisky Name:						
Type [x]:	Scotch [ ]	Irish [ ]	Other [ ]	Single Malt [ ]		Blend [ ]
	Bourbon [ ]	Rye [ ]	Single Pot [ ]	Corn [ ]		Barley [ ]
Region / Country:						
Distillery:						
Age:						
Strength %:						
Testing Date:						
Details:						

Whisky Name:					
Type [x]:	Scotch [ ]	Irish [ ]	Other [ ]	Single Malt [ ]	Blend [ ]
	Bourbon [ ]	Rye [ ]	Single Pot [ ]	Corn [ ]	Barley [ ]
Region / Country:					
Distillery:					
Age:					
Strength %:					
Testing Date:					
Details:					

Whisky Name:						
Type [x]:	Scotch [ ]	Irish [ ]	Other [ ]	Single Malt [ ]		Blend [ ]
	Bourbon [ ]	Rye [ ]	Single Pot [ ]	Corn [ ]		Barley [ ]
Region / Country:						
Distillery:						
Age:						
Strength %:						
Testing Date:						
Details:						

Whisky Name:					
Type [x]:	Scotch [ ]	Irish [ ]	Other [ ]	Single Malt [ ]	Blend [ ]
	Bourbon [ ]	Rye [ ]	Single Pot [ ]	Corn [ ]	Barley [ ]
Region / Country:					
Distillery:					
Age:					
Strength %:					
Testing Date:					
Details:					

Whisky Name:					
Type [x]:	Scotch [ ]	Irish [ ]	Other [ ]	Single Malt [ ]	Blend [ ]
	Bourbon [ ]	Rye [ ]	Single Pot [ ]	Corn [ ]	Barley [ ]
Region / Country:					
Distillery:					
Age:					
Strength %:					
Testing Date:					
Details:					

Whisky Name:					
Type [x]:	Scotch [ ]	Irish [ ]	Other [ ]	Single Malt [ ]	Blend [ ]
	Bourbon [ ]	Rye [ ]	Single Pot [ ]	Corn [ ]	Barley [ ]
Region / Country:					
Distillery:					
Age:					
Strength %:					
Testing Date:					
Details:					

Whisky Name:					
Type [x]:	Scotch [ ]	Irish [ ]	Other [ ]	Single Malt [ ]	Blend [ ]
	Bourbon [ ]	Rye [ ]	Single Pot [ ]	Corn [ ]	Barley [ ]
Region / Country:					
Distillery:					
Age:					
Strength %:					
Testing Date:					
Details:					

Whisky Name:					
Type [x]:	**Scotch [ ]**	**Irish [ ]**	**Other [ ]**	**Single Malt [ ]**	**Blend [ ]**
	Bourbon [ ]	**Rye [ ]**	**Single Pot [ ]**	**Corn [ ]**	**Barley [ ]**
Region / Country:					
Distillery:					
Age:					
Strength %:					
Testing Date:					
Details:					

Whisky Name:					
Type [x]:	Scotch [ ]	Irish [ ]	Other [ ]	Single Malt [ ]	Blend [ ]
	Bourbon [ ]	Rye [ ]	Single Pot [ ]	Corn [ ]	Barley [ ]
Region / Country:					
Distillery:					
Age:					
Strength %:					
Testing Date:					
Details:					

Whisky Name:					
Type [x]:	Scotch [ ]	Irish [ ]	Other [ ]	Single Malt [ ]	Blend [ ]
	Bourbon [ ]	Rye [ ]	Single Pot [ ]	Corn [ ]	Barley [ ]
Region / Country:					
Distillery:					
Age:					
Strength %:					
Testing Date:					
Details:					

Whisky Name:					
Type [x]:	Scotch [ ]	Irish [ ]	Other [ ]	Single Malt [ ]	Blend [ ]
	Bourbon [ ]	Rye [ ]	Single Pot [ ]	Corn [ ]	Barley [ ]
Region / Country:					
Distillery:					
Age:					
Strength %:					
Testing Date:					
Details:					

Whisky Name:					
Type [x]:	Scotch [ ]	Irish [ ]	Other [ ]	Single Malt [ ]	Blend [ ]
	Bourbon [ ]	Rye [ ]	Single Pot [ ]	Corn [ ]	Barley [ ]
Region / Country:					
Distillery:					
Age:					
Strength %:					
Testing Date:					
Details:					

Whisky Name:					
Type [x]:	Scotch [ ]	Irish [ ]	Other [ ]	Single Malt [ ]	Blend [ ]
	Bourbon [ ]	Rye [ ]	Single Pot [ ]	Corn [ ]	Barley [ ]
Region / Country:					
Distillery:					
Age:					
Strength %:					
Testing Date:					
Details:					

Whisky Name:						
Type [x]:	Scotch [ ]	Irish [ ]	Other [ ]	Single Malt [ ]	Blend [ ]
	Bourbon [ ]	Rye [ ]	Single Pot [ ]	Corn [ ]	Barley [ ]
Region / Country:						
Distillery:						
Age:						
Strength %:						
Testing Date:						
Details:						

Whisky Name:					
Type [x]:	Scotch [ ]	Irish [ ]	Other [ ]	Single Malt [ ]	Blend [ ]
	Bourbon [ ]	Rye [ ]	Single Pot [ ]	Corn [ ]	Barley [ ]
Region / Country:					
Distillery:					
Age:					
Strength %:					
Testing Date:					
Details:					

Whisky Name:					
Type [x]:	Scotch [ ]	Irish [ ]	Other [ ]	Single Malt [ ]	Blend [ ]
	Bourbon [ ]	Rye [ ]	Single Pot [ ]	Corn [ ]	Barley [ ]
Region / Country:					
Distillery:					
Age:					
Strength %:					
Testing Date:					
Details:					

Whisky Name:					
Type [x]:	Scotch [ ]	Irish [ ]	Other [ ]	Single Malt [ ]	Blend [ ]
	Bourbon [ ]	Rye [ ]	Single Pot [ ]	Corn [ ]	Barley [ ]
Region / Country:					
Distillery:					
Age:					
Strength %:					
Testing Date:					
Details:					

Whisky Name:					
Type [x]:	Scotch [ ]	Irish [ ]	Other [ ]	Single Malt [ ]	Blend [ ]
	Bourbon [ ]	Rye [ ]	Single Pot [ ]	Corn [ ]	Barley [ ]
Region / Country:					
Distillery:					
Age:					
Strength %:					
Testing Date:					
Details:					

Whisky Name:					
Type [x]:	Scotch [ ]	Irish [ ]	Other [ ]	Single Malt [ ]	Blend [ ]
	Bourbon [ ]	Rye [ ]	Single Pot [ ]	Corn [ ]	Barley [ ]
Region / Country:					
Distillery:					
Age:					
Strength %:					
Testing Date:					
Details:					

Whisky Name:					
Type [x]:	Scotch [ ]	Irish [ ]	Other [ ]	Single Malt [ ]	Blend [ ]
	Bourbon [ ]	Rye [ ]	Single Pot [ ]	Corn [ ]	Barley [ ]
Region / Country:					
Distillery:					
Age:					
Strength %:					
Testing Date:					
Details:					

Whisky Name:					
Type [x]:	Scotch [ ]	Irish [ ]	Other [ ] Single Malt [ ]		Blend [ ]
	Bourbon [ ]	Rye [ ]	Single Pot [ ] Corn [ ]		Barley [ ]
Region / Country:					
Distillery:					
Age:					
Strength %:					
Testing Date:					
Details:					

Whisky Name:					
Type [x]:	Scotch [ ]	Irish [ ]	Other [ ]	Single Malt [ ]	Blend [ ]
	Bourbon [ ]	Rye [ ]	Single Pot [ ]	Corn [ ]	Barley [ ]
Region / Country:					
Distillery:					
Age:					
Strength %:					
Testing Date:					
Details:					

Whisky Name:					
Type [x]:	Scotch [ ]	Irish [ ]	Other [ ]	Single Malt [ ]	Blend [ ]
	Bourbon [ ]	Rye [ ]	Single Pot [ ]	Corn [ ]	Barley [ ]
Region / Country:					
Distillery:					
Age:					
Strength %:					
Testing Date:					
Details:					

Whisky Name:					
Type [x]:	Scotch [ ]	Irish [ ]	Other [ ]	Single Malt [ ]	Blend [ ]
	Bourbon [ ]	Rye [ ]	Single Pot [ ]	Corn [ ]	Barley [ ]
Region / Country:					
Distillery:					
Age:					
Strength %:					
Testing Date:					
Details:					

Whisky Name:					
Type [x]:	Scotch [ ]	Irish [ ]	Other [ ]	Single Malt [ ]	Blend [ ]
	Bourbon [ ]	Rye [ ]	Single Pot [ ]	Corn [ ]	Barley [ ]
Region / Country:					
Distillery:					
Age:					
Strength %:					
Testing Date:					
Details:					

Whisky Name:						
Type [x]:	Scotch [ ]	Irish [ ]	Other [ ]	Single Malt [ ]		Blend [ ]
	Bourbon [ ]	Rye [ ]	Single Pot [ ]	Corn [ ]		Barley [ ]
Region / Country:						
Distillery:						
Age:						
Strength %:						
Testing Date:						
Details:						

Whisky Name:					
Type [x]:	Scotch [ ]	Irish [ ]	Other [ ]	Single Malt [ ]	Blend [ ]
	Bourbon [ ]	Rye [ ]	Single Pot [ ]	Corn [ ]	Barley [ ]
Region / Country:					
Distillery:					
Age:					
Strength %:					
Testing Date:					
Details:					

Whisky Name:					
Type [x]:	Scotch [ ]	Irish [ ]	Other [ ]	Single Malt [ ]	Blend [ ]
	Bourbon [ ]	Rye [ ]	Single Pot [ ]	Corn [ ]	Barley [ ]
Region / Country:					
Distillery:					
Age:					
Strength %:					
Testing Date:					
Details:					

Whisky Name:					
Type [x]:	Scotch [ ]	Irish [ ]	Other [ ]	Single Malt [ ]	Blend [ ]
	Bourbon [ ]	Rye [ ]	Single Pot [ ]	Corn [ ]	Barley [ ]
Region / Country:					
Distillery:					
Age:					
Strength %:					
Testing Date:					
Details:					

Whisky Name:					
Type [x]:	Scotch [ ]	Irish [ ]	Other [ ]	Single Malt [ ]	Blend [ ]
	Bourbon [ ]	Rye [ ]	Single Pot [ ]	Corn [ ]	Barley [ ]
Region / Country:					
Distillery:					
Age:					
Strength %:					
Testing Date:					
Details:					

Whisky Name:					
Type [x]:	Scotch [ ]	Irish [ ]	Other [ ]	Single Malt [ ]	Blend [ ]
	Bourbon [ ]	Rye [ ]	Single Pot [ ]	Corn [ ]	Barley [ ]
Region / Country:					
Distillery:					
Age:					
Strength %:					
Testing Date:					
Details:					

Whisky Name:					
Type [x]:	Scotch [ ]	Irish [ ]	Other [ ]	Single Malt [ ]	Blend [ ]
	Bourbon [ ]	Rye [ ]	Single Pot [ ]	Corn [ ]	Barley [ ]
Region / Country:					
Distillery:					
Age:					
Strength %:					
Testing Date:					
Details:					

Whisky Name:					
Type [x]:	Scotch [ ]	Irish [ ]	Other [ ]	Single Malt [ ]	Blend [ ]
	Bourbon [ ]	Rye [ ]	Single Pot [ ]	Corn [ ]	Barley [ ]
Region / Country:					
Distillery:					
Age:					
Strength %:					
Testing Date:					
Details:					

Whisky Name:						
Type [x]:	Scotch [ ]	Irish [ ]	Other [ ]	Single Malt [ ]		Blend [ ]
	Bourbon [ ]	Rye [ ]	Single Pot [ ]	Corn [ ]		Barley [ ]
Region / Country:						
Distillery:						
Age:						
Strength %:						
Testing Date:						
Details:						

Whisky Name:					
Type [x]:	Scotch [ ]	Irish [ ]	Other [ ]	Single Malt [ ]	Blend [ ]
	Bourbon [ ]	Rye [ ]	Single Pot [ ]	Corn [ ]	Barley [ ]
Region / Country:					
Distillery:					
Age:					
Strength %:					
Testing Date:					
Details:					

Whisky Name:					
Type [x]:	Scotch [ ]	Irish [ ]	Other [ ]	Single Malt [ ]	Blend [ ]
	Bourbon [ ]	Rye [ ]	Single Pot [ ]	Corn [ ]	Barley [ ]
Region / Country:					
Distillery:					
Age:					
Strength %:					
Testing Date:					
Details:					

Whisky Name:					
Type [x]:	Scotch [ ]	Irish [ ]	Other [ ]	Single Malt [ ]	Blend [ ]
	Bourbon [ ]	Rye [ ]	Single Pot [ ]	Corn [ ]	Barley [ ]
Region / Country:					
Distillery:					
Age:					
Strength %:					
Testing Date:					
Details:					

Whisky Name:					
Type [x]:	Scotch [ ]	Irish [ ]	Other [ ]	Single Malt [ ]	Blend [ ]
	Bourbon [ ]	Rye [ ]	Single Pot [ ]	Corn [ ]	Barley [ ]
Region / Country:					
Distillery:					
Age:					
Strength %:					
Testing Date:					
Details:					

Whisky Name:					
Type [x]:	Scotch [ ]	Irish [ ]	Other [ ]	Single Malt [ ]	Blend [ ]
	Bourbon [ ]	Rye [ ]	Single Pot [ ]	Corn [ ]	Barley [ ]
Region / Country:					
Distillery:					
Age:					
Strength %:					
Testing Date:					
Details:					

Whisky Name:					
Type [x]:	Scotch [ ]	Irish [ ]	Other [ ]	Single Malt [ ]	Blend [ ]
	Bourbon [ ]	Rye [ ]	Single Pot [ ]	Corn [ ]	Barley [ ]
Region / Country:					
Distillery:					
Age:					
Strength %:					
Testing Date:					
Details:					

Whisky Name:					
Type [x]:	Scotch [ ]	Irish [ ]	Other [ ]	Single Malt [ ]	Blend [ ]
	Bourbon [ ]	Rye [ ]	Single Pot [ ]	Corn [ ]	Barley [ ]
Region / Country:					
Distillery:					
Age:					
Strength %:					
Testing Date:					
Details:					

Whisky Name:						
Type [x]:	Scotch [ ]	Irish [ ]	Other [ ]	Single Malt [ ]	Blend [ ]	
	Bourbon [ ]	Rye [ ]	Single Pot [ ]	Corn [ ]	Barley [ ]	
Region / Country:						
Distillery:						
Age:						
Strength %:						
Testing Date:						
Details:						

Whisky Name:					
Type [x]:	Scotch [ ]	Irish [ ]	Other [ ]	Single Malt [ ]	Blend [ ]
	Bourbon [ ]	Rye [ ]	Single Pot [ ]	Corn [ ]	Barley [ ]
Region / Country:					
Distillery:					
Age:					
Strength %:					
Testing Date:					
Details:					

Whisky Name:					
Type [x]:	Scotch [ ]	Irish [ ]	Other [ ]	Single Malt [ ]	Blend [ ]
	Bourbon [ ]	Rye [ ]	Single Pot [ ]	Corn [ ]	Barley [ ]
Region / Country:					
Distillery:					
Age:					
Strength %:					
Testing Date:					
Details:					

Whisky Name:					
Type [x]:	Scotch [ ]	Irish [ ]	Other [ ] Single Malt [ ]		Blend [ ]
	Bourbon [ ]	Rye [ ]	Single Pot [ ]	Corn [ ]	Barley [ ]
Region / Country:					
Distillery:					
Age:					
Strength %:					
Testing Date:					
Details:					

Whisky Name:					
Type [x]:	Scotch [ ]	Irish [ ]	Other [ ]	Single Malt [ ]	Blend [ ]
	Bourbon [ ]	Rye [ ]	Single Pot [ ]	Corn [ ]	Barley [ ]
Region / Country:					
Distillery:					
Age:					
Strength %:					
Testing Date:					
Details:					

Whisky Name:					
Type [x]:	Scotch [ ]	Irish [ ]	Other [ ]	Single Malt [ ]	Blend [ ]
	Bourbon [ ]	Rye [ ]	Single Pot [ ]	Corn [ ]	Barley [ ]
Region / Country:					
Distillery:					
Age:					
Strength %:					
Testing Date:					
Details:					

Whisky Name:						
Type [x]:	Scotch [ ]	Irish [ ]	Other [ ]	Single Malt [ ]		Blend [ ]
	Bourbon [ ]	Rye [ ]	Single Pot [ ]	Corn [ ]		Barley [ ]
Region / Country:						
Distillery:						
Age:						
Strength %:						
Testing Date:						
Details:						

Whisky Name:						
Type [x]:	Scotch [ ]	Irish [ ]	Other [ ]	Single Malt [ ]		Blend [ ]
	Bourbon [ ]	Rye [ ]	Single Pot [ ]	Corn [ ]		Barley [ ]
Region / Country:						
Distillery:						
Age:						
Strength %:						
Testing Date:						
Details:						

Whisky Name:					
Type [x]:	Scotch [ ]	Irish [ ]	Other [ ]	Single Malt [ ]	Blend [ ]
	Bourbon [ ]	Rye [ ]	Single Pot [ ]	Corn [ ]	Barley [ ]
Region / Country:					
Distillery:					
Age:					
Strength %:					
Testing Date:					
Details:					

Whisky Name:					
Type [x]:	Scotch [ ]	Irish [ ]	Other [ ]	Single Malt [ ]	Blend [ ]
	Bourbon [ ]	Rye [ ]	Single Pot [ ]	Corn [ ]	Barley [ ]
Region / Country:					
Distillery:					
Age:					
Strength %:					
Testing Date:					
Details:					

Whisky Name:					
Type [x]:	Scotch [ ]	Irish [ ]	Other [ ]	Single Malt [ ]	Blend [ ]
	Bourbon [ ]	Rye [ ]	Single Pot [ ]	Corn [ ]	Barley [ ]
Region / Country:					
Distillery:					
Age:					
Strength %:					
Testing Date:					
Details:					

Whisky Name:					
Type [x]:	Scotch [ ]	Irish [ ]	Other [ ]	Single Malt [ ]	Blend [ ]
	Bourbon [ ]	Rye [ ]	Single Pot [ ]	Corn [ ]	Barley [ ]
Region / Country:					
Distillery:					
Age:					
Strength %:					
Testing Date:					
Details:					

Whisky Name:					
Type [x]:	Scotch [ ]	Irish [ ]	Other [ ]	Single Malt [ ]	Blend [ ]
	Bourbon [ ]	Rye [ ]	Single Pot [ ]	Corn [ ]	Barley [ ]
Region / Country:					
Distillery:					
Age:					
Strength %:					
Testing Date:					
Details:					

Whisky Name:					
Type [x]:	Scotch [ ]	Irish [ ]	Other [ ]	Single Malt [ ]	Blend [ ]
	Bourbon [ ]	Rye [ ]	Single Pot [ ]	Corn [ ]	Barley [ ]
Region / Country:					
Distillery:					
Age:					
Strength %:					
Testing Date:					
Details:					

Whisky Name:					
Type [x]:	Scotch [ ]	Irish [ ]	Other [ ]	Single Malt [ ]	Blend [ ]
	Bourbon [ ]	Rye [ ]	Single Pot [ ]	Corn [ ]	Barley [ ]
Region / Country:					
Distillery:					
Age:					
Strength %:					
Testing Date:					
Details:					

Whisky Name:					
Type [x]:	Scotch [ ]	Irish [ ]	Other [ ]	Single Malt [ ]	Blend [ ]
	Bourbon [ ]	Rye [ ]	Single Pot [ ]	Corn [ ]	Barley [ ]
Region / Country:					
Distillery:					
Age:					
Strength %:					
Testing Date:					
Details:					

Whisky Name:						
Type [x]:	Scotch [ ]	Irish [ ]	Other [ ]	Single Malt [ ]		Blend [ ]
	Bourbon [ ]	Rye [ ]	Single Pot [ ]	Corn [ ]		Barley [ ]
Region / Country:						
Distillery:						
Age:						
Strength %:						
Testing Date:						
Details:						

Whisky Name:					
Type [x]:	Scotch [ ]	Irish [ ]	Other [ ]	Single Malt [ ]	Blend [ ]
	Bourbon [ ]	Rye [ ]	Single Pot [ ]	Corn [ ]	Barley [ ]
Region / Country:					
Distillery:					
Age:					
Strength %:					
Testing Date:					
Details:					

Whisky Name:					
Type [x]:	Scotch [ ]	Irish [ ]	Other [ ]	Single Malt [ ]	Blend [ ]
	Bourbon [ ]	Rye [ ]	Single Pot [ ]	Corn [ ]	Barley [ ]
Region / Country:					
Distillery:					
Age:					
Strength %:					
Testing Date:					
Details:					

Whisky Name:					
Type [x]:	Scotch [ ]	Irish [ ]	Other [ ]	Single Malt [ ]	Blend [ ]
	Bourbon [ ]	Rye [ ]	Single Pot [ ]	Corn [ ]	Barley [ ]
Region / Country:					
Distillery:					
Age:					
Strength %:					
Testing Date:					
Details:					

Whisky Name:					
Type [x]:	Scotch [ ]	Irish [ ]	Other [ ]	Single Malt [ ]	Blend [ ]
	Bourbon [ ]	Rye [ ]	Single Pot [ ]	Corn [ ]	Barley [ ]
Region / Country:					
Distillery:					
Age:					
Strength %:					
Testing Date:					
Details:					

Whisky Name:					
Type [x]:	Scotch [ ]	Irish [ ]	Other [ ]	Single Malt [ ]	Blend [ ]
	Bourbon [ ]	Rye [ ]	Single Pot [ ]	Corn [ ]	Barley [ ]
Region / Country:					
Distillery:					
Age:					
Strength %:					
Testing Date:					
Details:					

Whisky Name:						
Type [x]:	Scotch [ ]	Irish [ ]	Other [ ]	Single Malt [ ]		Blend [ ]
	Bourbon [ ]	Rye [ ]	Single Pot [ ]	Corn [ ]		Barley [ ]
Region / Country:						
Distillery:						
Age:						
Strength %:						
Testing Date:						
Details:						

Whisky Name:						
Type [x]:	Scotch [ ]	Irish [ ]	Other [ ]	Single Malt [ ]		Blend [ ]
	Bourbon [ ]	Rye [ ]	Single Pot [ ]	Corn [ ]		Barley [ ]
Region / Country:						
Distillery:						
Age:						
Strength %:						
Testing Date:						
Details:						

Whisky Name:						
Type [x]:	Scotch [ ]	Irish [ ]	Other [ ]	Single Malt [ ]		Blend [ ]
	Bourbon [ ]	Rye [ ]	Single Pot [ ]	Corn [ ]		Barley [ ]
Region / Country:						
Distillery:						
Age:						
Strength %:						
Testing Date:						
Details:						

Whisky Name:					
Type [x]:	Scotch [ ]	Irish [ ]	Other [ ]	Single Malt [ ]	Blend [ ]
	Bourbon [ ]	Rye [ ]	Single Pot [ ]	Corn [ ]	Barley [ ]
Region / Country:					
Distillery:					
Age:					
Strength %:					
Testing Date:					
Details:					

Whisky Name:					
Type [x]:	Scotch [ ]	Irish [ ]	Other [ ]	Single Malt [ ]	Blend [ ]
	Bourbon [ ]	Rye [ ]	Single Pot [ ]	Corn [ ]	Barley [ ]
Region / Country:					
Distillery:					
Age:					
Strength %:					
Testing Date:					
Details:					

Whisky Name:					
Type [x]:	Scotch [ ]	Irish [ ]	Other [ ]	Single Malt [ ]	Blend [ ]
	Bourbon [ ]	Rye [ ]	Single Pot [ ]	Corn [ ]	Barley [ ]
Region / Country:					
Distillery:					
Age:					
Strength %:					
Testing Date:					
Details:					

Whisky Name:						
Type [x]:	Scotch [ ]	Irish [ ]	Other [ ]	Single Malt [ ]		Blend [ ]
	Bourbon [ ]	Rye [ ]	Single Pot [ ]	Corn [ ]		Barley [ ]
Region / Country:						
Distillery:						
Age:						
Strength %:						
Testing Date:						
Details:						

Whisky Name:					
Type [x]:	Scotch [ ]	Irish [ ]	Other [ ]	Single Malt [ ]	Blend [ ]
	Bourbon [ ]	Rye [ ]	Single Pot [ ]	Corn [ ]	Barley [ ]
Region / Country:					
Distillery:					
Age:					
Strength %:					
Testing Date:					
Details:					

Made in the USA
Monee, IL
04 December 2020